School

by Linda Cave
illustrated by Gary Undercuffler

Pre-Decodable 5

McGraw Hill Education

Bothell, WA • Chicago, IL • Columbus, OH • New York, NY

MHEonline.com

Send all inquiries to:
McGraw-Hill Education
8787 Orion Place
Columbus, OH 43240

ISBN: 978-0-02-146205-6
MHID: 0-02-146205-4

Printed in the United States of America.

11 12 13 LCR 25 24 23

a  and a 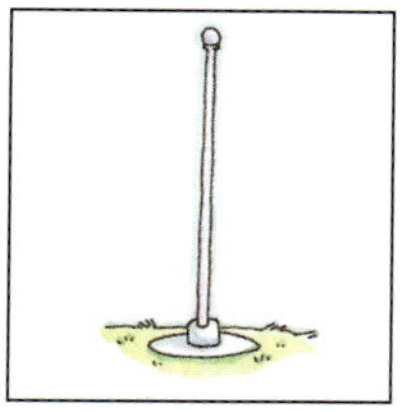

flag pole

the  and 

boys girls

the  and 

tables

chairs

the

books

and

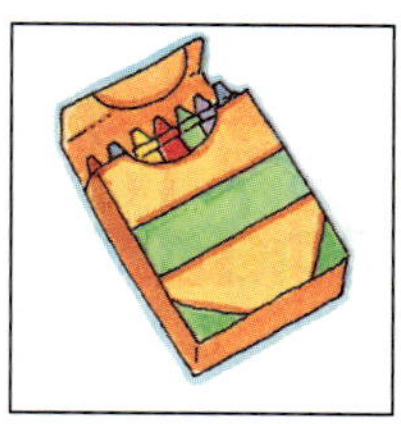

crayons

a 

board

and a 

teacher

the  school and  students